MORT GREENBERG

REVENUE
BOOST

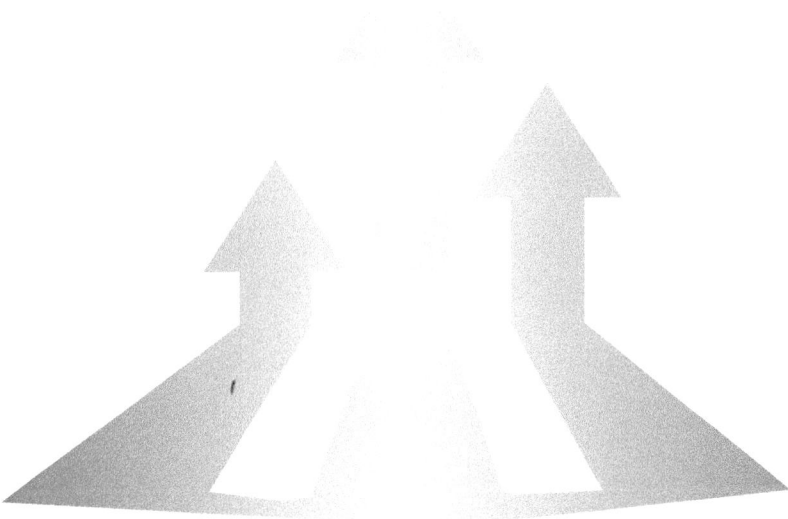

THE ULTIMATE SALES PLAN IN FIVE STEPS

OTHER BOOKS
BY <u>MORT GREENBERG</u>

THE SINGULAR FOCUS
100+ Tips to Maximize Your Revenue

STRAIGHT UP SELLING
Your Toolbox for Sales Excellence

What Others Are Saying About the Author

Kenny Wachtel | Formerly SVP of Sales for Excite@Home

One day back in 1997, Mort, who I had just promoted to Sales AE, approached me as the CRO at an early internet startup named Excite, and told me that we should buy a small company called eBay. They weren't on anybody's radar back then. This is the kind of guy that Mort is – able to peer into the future and bring potential opportunities into the present. Due to the efforts of sales executives like Mort, Excite grew its valuation from $100 million to over $6.7 billion at merger 3 years later. A go-getter, closer extraordinaire, and future forecaster all wrapped in one package. I wish that I had more Morts on the staff.

Matt Gilbert | Former SVP IAC / InterActive Corp and current CEO of Partnerize.

When it comes to building a sales organization capable of sustained excellence, there is no better architect than Mort. Revenue Boost captures the key pillars upon which Mort enabled tens of millions of dollars in sales with the type of cost efficiency that makes CFO's smile. Over a 5-year period at Ask Jeeves, Mort's approach underpinned a turnaround effort that materially contributed to a valuation increase from $33M to an exit to IAC / InterActive Corp of $2B. Following the acquisition, Mort's playbook was the foundation for the creation of IAC Advertising Solutions, a business unit that was responsible for the monetization of all advertising inventory across a portfolio including Ask.com, Expedia, CitySearch, Ticketmaster, Evite, Match.com, Lending Tree and more.

Allen Blum | Former SVP Time Warner, VP NBCUniversal. Now Head of Revenue & Partnerships at Foiye

During Mort's time at NBCU, he was a key part of rebuilding the local television station group's push towards online and mobile platforms. Very often we would partner to create first & one-of-a-kind ways for brands to leverage both linear and digital to maximize their message and therefore attain their value propositions on a variety of geo-targeted platforms. Arguably, the NBC owned and operated station group covered the largest DMAs in the country and delivered 1+ billion dollars of revenue to the company's portfolio.

Kevin Dulsky | Formerly Nokia's Head of Global Mobile Advertising. Currently Partner Andreessen Horowitz

I was fortunate to have Mort as part of my leadership team. It was inspiring watching him run around the globe and motivate those on his team and win over clients new and old. He is an exceptional sales leader, and skilled communicator who can clearly articulate complex ideas. Mort's efforts and positive ways helped us navigate change in our division as Microsoft acquired Nokia's devices and services businesses.

Kevin Dorsey | Formerly President of National Media Groups, iHeartMedia. Now running his own media and digital advisory firm

Once Clear Channel obtained Department of Justice clearance for the acquisition of Westwood One's Metro Traffic division Mort ran the day-to-day process to integrate this unit with our wholly owned subsidiary Total Traffic Network and lead our sales team. The combination of two $100M+ businesses into one became Total Traffic + Weather Network.

REVENUE BOOST

The Ultimate Sales Plan in Five Steps

digitalCORE
PUBLISHING

DIGITALCORE PUBLISHING

First Paperback edition December 2022

ISBN: 979-8-9873618-6-3 (eBook)

ISBN: ISBN: 979-8-9873618-5-6 (Print)

Published by digitalCORE, Inc.

http://dgtlcore.com/

FOR EVERYONE
THAT SELLS FOR A LIVING
AND WOULD LIKE TO IMPROVE
THEIR CRAFT

REVENUE.
MINDSET.

AUTHOR'S NOTE

Early in my career the Silicon Valley corporate world that openly embraced me always placed business school graduates in the top jobs. Looking closer at how these grads operated two items jumped out: First, they were great listeners, highly analytical, and asked the best questions. Second, they were great managers of their time, and no matter how hard they worked they always found ways to take vacations, and not work on the weekends.

For me, business school was never going to be in the cards. So the next best thing was to learn as much as possible from business school graduates who attended Harvard, Stanford, Wharton, Columbia, and more.

Week after week, part of the challenge set in my head was that no one would put in more hours than I would. Many nights that meant being in the office until 10 PM or later, and half-day Saturdays and Sundays at a minimum.

This to me was the only way to get ahead of my co-workers, and to continually find more customers and generate more revenue. Canceling planned vacations happened all too often but my view was that I was in learning mode.

For a few years, I worked for NBC Universal while General Electric owned the company. Each year we had a four-phase planning effort that ran throughout the year: Session C in February, with the Chairman of each business unit to review each employee and the business overall, Session 1 (S1) in May, to review performance so far in the year, Session 2 (S2) in September, to see how the year would finish and Growth Playbook (GPB) in October, to build next year's expansion plan. The cadence to make planning part of every quarter during the year paid dividends in our growth and ability to stay ahead of the competition.

Every Fall, most companies begin a strategic planning process for the next calendar year. They may not run a process as involved as NBC and GE, but they do put in the effort. Wondering how to create the simplest but most impactful plan is part of where the idea for this book came from. My eagerness to keep learning from anyone that would talk with me about strategic planning has never faded. Paul Gardi and Johnsie Garrett, in many ways this book was made possible because of the time and effort you spent with me over many years. First, you showed me how to bring together objectives, goals, strategies, measures, and tactics. Then you helped me understand each word that goes into the OGSMT is critically important and should be questioned.

This book is built in the form of a workbook. The goal of this workbook is to provide a path to create a simple, but detailed plan to beat your revenue target. These steps can also be used to create a strategic plan for departments beyond sales. However, in a world where sellers must focus on providing customers with the best service and at the same time deliver on their revenue targets, getting lost in planning is rarely an option. This is a do-it-yourself, write in the book to get your ideas on paper. Then scan the QR code to copy the Google Sheets Workbook to your Google Drive and type up your new plan.

Workbook Overview

COURSE INCLUDES COMPANION WORKSHEETS + GOOGLE SHEET WORKBOOK

INTRODUCTION

- **OBJECTIVE:** [WHAT TO ACCOMPLISH]
  Develop Your Revenue Mindset

- **MISSION:** [PURPOSE]
  Improve Your Business Outcomes

1

Make Everyone Feel Like an Insider

THE SURVEY

3

Build A Map To Beat Your Competition

COMPETITIVE FACTORS

4

Strengths.
Weaknesses.
Opportunities.
Threats

THE S.W.O.T

2

Your Business On
One Page

BUSINESS CANVAS

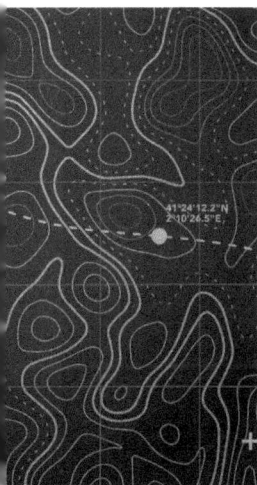

5

Objectives. Goals. Strategies. Measures. Tactics.

THE OGSMT

TABLE OF CONTENTS

Three Benefits
of This Book

01. **02.** **03.**

Access New Tools To Grow Your Revenue Mindset	Learn The Five Step Process for Writing Simple but Effective Plans	Integrate Relentless Preparation Into Your Routine

INTRODUCTION

- **OBJECTIVE:** [WHAT TO ACCOMPLISH]
  Develop Your Revenue Mindset

- **MISSION:** [PURPOSE]
  Improve Your Business Outcomes

Why Have A Written Sales Plan?

MANAGE & MAKE THE MOST OF YOUR TIME

WRITE FAST.

SET, TRACK & BEAT
YOUR GOALS!

RETREAT. REPEAT.

The Five Step Process > Series of One Sheets

1. SURVEY > 2. BUSINESS CANVAS > 3.COMPETITOR GRID
> 4. SWOT > 5. OGSMT

OGSMT
20XX

Mission (Purpose)

Vision (Aspiration)

THE WHAT		THE HOW				
O - OBJECTIVES	G - GOALS	S - STRAGTEGIES	M - MEASURES	T - TACTICS	OWNER(S)	DUE DATE
What to Accomplish / Overarching, qualitative goals for the business	Quantitative Measures That Define Success	Plans to Bring Achievement of Quantitative Goals	Date or Numerical Metric of Success of Strategy	Actions / Projects Needed to Complete Strategy	Owner of Tactic	Target Date for Completion of Tactic
	G1	S1	M1	T1 / T2	U1 / U2	D1 / D2
			M2	T3 / T4	U3 / U4	D3 / D4
		S2	M3	T5 / T6	U5 / U6	D5 / D6
O2	G2	S3	M4	T7 / T8	U7 / U8	D7 / D8
			M5	T9 / T10	U9 / U10	D9 / D10
		S4	M6	T11 / T12	U11 / U12	D11 / D12
O3	G3	S5	M7	T13 / T14	U13 / U14	D13 / D14
			M8	T15 / T16	U15 / U16	D15 / D16
		S6	M9	T17 / T18	U17 / U18	D17 / D18

Please scan the QR code to access the Google Sheets and Excel Workbook. For Google Sheets, the file is in "View" mode so choose "File", "Copy" and then save it to your G Drive to edit

1

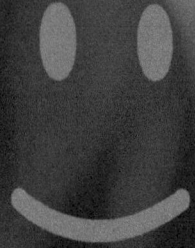

Make Everyone Feel Like an Insider

THE SURVEY

Prepare Your Team For Sales Planning

Let everyone know that you are beginning a strategic planning process

Have everyone complete a survey you will be sending around

Tell everyone that it will be a transparent process and they will all be involved

That all will see the survey results and this information will be part of your plan

And that once the plan starts coming together it will be shared in small groups

Capturing Survey Data

GOOGLE

FORMS

OR

SURVEY

MONKEY

Example Survey Questions

- What do you like most about our product(s)?

- What improvement is needed for our product(s)?

- How would you rate our customer service?

- Are we consistent and repeatable in the results our products deliver to you?

- Which of our competitors do you like working with and why?

- What else can we do to improve?

- Other thoughts you would like to share?

CAPTURE FEEDBACK FROM AS MANY PEOPLE AS YOU CAN

- What do you like most at "company name"?

- What needs to improve at "company name"?

- Who do you view as our competitors?

- What products need improvement? Why?

- What new products should we offer?

- What do you think can help grow sales?

- What tools do you need to do your job?

- Other thoughts or comments?

Once You Have Your Response Submissions...

☑ Review to see common themes

📊 Prioritize items based on volume of similar responses

▦ Place items into Excel grid in priority order

💬 Share Employee and Customer feedback with team *(No need to share customer feedback with customers)*

BUILD AND SEND OUT YOUR SURVEY

☑ Write 7+/- Customer Survey Questions

☑ Write 7+/- Employee Survey Questions

☑ Explore Google Forms (Free) &

SurveyMonkey ($25 / Mo. & Up)

☑ Write Your Survey

☑ Send Out Your Survey

Customer Questions

1. _____

2. _____

3. _____

4. _____

5. _____

6. _____

7. _____

8. _____

9. _____

10. _____

Employee Questions

1. _____

2. _____

3. _____

4. _____

5. _____

6. _____

7. _____

8. _____

9. _____

10. _____

2

Your Business On
One Page

BUSINESS CANVAS

Nine Elements of Your Business Canvas

1. Business Specialty

2. Why Customers Work With You

3. Key Vendors

4. Key Customer Segments

5. Relationship Customers Want

6. Key Resources (Have & Need)

7. Growth Areas

8. Cost Structure

9. Revenue Streams

[PLACE YOUR LOGO HERE]

Business Specialty	Reasons Custome
What do we do? What is Product Set?	*Which customer proble*

Key Customer Segments	Relationship Custom
For whom are we creating value?, Who are our most important customers?	*What type of relationship does each Cust & maint*

Growth Areas to Drive New Revenue	Costs Str
What Channels, Platforms Are Missing or Need Improvement?	*What are ou*

Business Canvas
20XX

rs Work with Us	Key Vendors
ns are we solving?	Who are our top suppliers? What activities does each perform?

ners Want with Us	Key Resources (Have & Need)
omer Segment expect us to establish ain?	What resources do we need to deliver value to our customers? What do we need that we do not have?

ucture	Revenue Streams
r Costs?	What are our Revenue Streams?

Value of Your Business Canvas

- Forces you to think through what you do

- Allows you to simplify writing your business plan

- Helps prioritize who your customers are

HELPFUL TIP: Having a basic P&L completed before completing your business canvas will help answer last two grid items

WRITE YOUR BUSINESS CANVAS

☑ Fill in as much info as you can in your business canvas

☑ Make sure you have your P&L or draft a high-level set of financials

☑ Sit back and congratulate yourself once all nine boxes are filled in!

☑ Version this and know it could take 8 or 10 versions to get right

1. Business Speciality	2. Why Customers Work W/ You
4. Key Customer Segments	5. Relationship Customers Want
7. Growth Areas	8. Cost Structure

	3. Key Vendors
	6. Key Resources (Have & Need)
	9. Revenue Streams

3

Build A Map To Beat

Your Competition

COMPETITIVE
FACTORS

Define Your Factors of competition

1. List out 3 – 10 Factors

2. Example Factors on Next Page are for a
   Media Company

3. Get data points for Your Company and
   Top 3 Competitors

4. Prioritize Areas of Improvement

5. Create New Benchmarks to Set as Goals
   for Your Company

[PLACE YOUR LOGO HERE]

Key Stats / Factors of Competition	Your Company
# Total Visits	
Avg. Visit Duration	
# Pages per Visit	
Have Print	
Facebook Followers	
Instagram Followers	
Tik Tok Followers	
YouTube Followers	

Top Competitors
20XX

Competitor 1	Competitor 2	Competitor 3

BENCHMARK WITH FACTORS OF COMPETITION

☑ Determine your top 3 competitors

☑ List out 3 -10 items you compete on

☑ Build your grid and see how you stack up

☑ Note what items you need to improve on

Competitor 1	Factor 1
Competitor 2	Factor 2
Competitor 3	Factor 3

	Factor 4
	Factor 5
	Factor 6

4

41°24'12.2
2°10'26.5"

Strengths. Weaknesses.
Opportunities. Threats

THE S.W.O.T

List Your Strengths, Weaknesses, Opportunities & Threats

- SWOT analysis helps identify Strengths, Weaknesses, Opportunities, and Threats

- This version allows you to find "Internal" Strengths and Weaknesses

- And also find "External" Opportunities and Threats

[PLACE YOUR LOGO HERE]

	STRENGTHS
INTERNAL	1)
	2)
	3)
	4)
	5)

	OPPORTUNITIES
EXTERNAL	1)
	2)
	3)
	4)
	5)

SWOT
20XX

WEAKNESSES

1)

2)

3)

4)

5)

THREATS

1)

2)

3)

4)

5)

TASK #4

COLLECT YOUR SWOT INPUT

☑ Use your customer survey responses to find external items

☑ Use your employee survey responses to help with internal items

Strengths (Internal)	Weaknesses (Internal)
Opportunities (External)	Threats (External)

1 2

Steps 1-4 Prepare You to Author Your Strategic Plan

3.4

Step 5 – The End Goal is to Write Your O.G.S.M.T

5

Objectives. Goals.
Strategies. Measures.

Tactics.

THE OGSMT

One Sheet Long Term Plan

- WHAT you want to achieve and HOW you are going to achieve it.

- OGSMT links long-term (Mission, Vision and Objectives) to short- and medium-term (Goals, Strategies, Measures and Tactics)

- Use your OGSMT to monitor progress toward your beating your revenue targets and maintain focus!

[PLACE YOUR LOGO HERE]

Mission (Purpose)

Vision (Aspiration)

THE WHAT		
O - OBJECTIVES	**G - GOALS**	**S - STRAGTEGIES**
What to Accomplish / Overarching, qualitative goals for the business	Quantitative Measures That Define Success	Plans to Bring Achievement of Quantitative Goals
O1	G1	S1 S2
O2	G2	S3 S4
O3	G3	S5 S6

THE HOW			
M - MEASURES	**T - TACTICS**	**OWNER(S)**	**DUE DATE**
Date or Numerical Metric of Success of Strategy	*Actions / Projects Needed to Complete Strategy*	*Owner of Tactic*	*Target Date for Completion of Tactic*
M1	T1	U1	D1
	T2	U2	D2
M2	T3	U3	D3
	T4	U4	D4
M3	T5	U5	D5
	T6	U6	D6
M4	T7	U7	D7
	T8	U8	D8
M5	T9	U9	D9
	T10	U10	D10
M6	T11	U11	D11
	T12	U12	D12
M7	T13	U13	D13
	T14	U14	D14
M8	T15	U15	D15
	T16	U16	D16
M9	T17	U17	D17
	T18	U18	D18

Formatting Your OGSMT

OBJECTIVES	GOALS	STRATEGIES
Long term, broad objective(s) – usually to be accomplished over the next year+ What we need/want to fulfill mandate or mission Your objectives should be obvious and simple.	Covers large, overriding considerations such as Revenue, Share, Volume, and Profit. The specific results we need to achieve our objective A specific and actionable definition of what 'success' looks like. Must be S.M.A.R.T. (Specific, measurable, actionable, realistic, time-bound.)	The key 4-5 strategies designed to build the competitive advantage necessary to achieve the goals. How we will achieve our goals Often take the form of projects or programs. Must make a specific decision or it is not a strategy.
Words	**Numbers/Dates**	**Words**

MEASURES	TACTICS
That which tells you that the strategies are being achieved (specific benchmarks, usually with a one-year horizon). Objective and quantifiable. Necessitates data collection. Measures serve as the basis for evaluating performance of the organization and of the managers, volunteers and employees.	Specific list of projects that as completed will bring you closer to achieving your strategies. Each of the 4-5 strategies will have 5-10, or more tactics
Numbers	**Words**

What Is Your Mission Statement?

Mission statements express:
1. Organization / team's purpose
2. Why you exist

SHORTER THE BETTER

GOOGLE: Organize the world's information and make it universally accessible and useful.

TESLA To accelerate the world's transition to sustainable energy.

BOEING: Open new frontiers.

TED: Spread ideas.

What Is Your Vision Statement? 5b

Vision statements express:
1. Future-focused, Dream big
2. Infuse with passion and emotion

SHORTER THE BETTER

GOOGLE: To provide access to the world's information in one click.

TESLA: Accelerate the advent of sustainable transport by bringing mass-market electric cars to market as soon as possible.

BOEING: People working together as a global enterprise for aerospace Leadership

TED: We believe passionately in the power of ideas to change attitudes, lives, and, ultimately, the world.

The Five Elements Of The OGSMT

OG- "WHAT" needs to be done

- Objective(s)
- Written statement of compelling business needs

- Goals
- Numerical target and scorecard to track progress toward meeting objectives

5c 5d 5e 5f 5g

SMT- "HOW" you will achieve your objectives

- Strategies
- Written statement of specific actions that must be taken to meet objectives

- Measures
- Numerical measures to track progress on executing specific actions

- Tactics
- Specific projects that need to be accomplished

Setting **Objectives**
(What To Accomplish)

Your Objectives Set The Direction For Your
Organization And Show What You Need To
Accomplish

**An effective Objective statement shows where
the business is headed. Your objectives describes
the ambition of your business and answer two
questions:**

> 1. What are your trying to achieve?
> 2. What does success look like?

WHEN WRITING YOUR OBJECTIVES THINK ABOUT

- What do others rely on you / your team / your company for?
- What needs to improve in your group next year, and year after...

EXAMPLE OBJECTIVES

- Grow Revenue Year over Year
- Set Industry Standard for Customer Service
- Create outreach to convert non-spending prospects to customers
- Launch Sales and Leadership Academy to Improve Team Skills

TAKE FIRST PASS AT WRITING 2-4 OBJECTIVES

• Objective 1:

• Objective 2:

• Objective 3:

• Objective 4:

YOUR GOALS ARE NUMBERS THAT DEFINE HIGH LEVEL SUCCESS WEEKLY, MONTHLY, QUARTERLY AND ANNUALLY

Your Goals are financial and / or operational and make your Objectives visible in measurable terms and answer two questions:

1. What must we accomplish financially
2. What must we accomplish numerically?

WHEN WRITING YOUR GOALS THINK ABOUT

- What are the key metrics of your industry and competitors?
- What metrics can be used to evaluate each employee?
- What metrics are possible to achieve next year?

EXAMPLE GOALS

- Annual sales of $50M+ (7% $ Growth over last year): Goals by Q: Q1 $5.0M, Q2 $10.0M, Q3 $15M, Q4 $20M
- Capture 20% of all spend in our space
- Work with 350+ customers this year

TAKE FIRST PASS AT WRITING GOALS

- **Weekly goals:**
  - Revenue & Profit
  - % Share
  - Volume of Clients / Contracts

- **Monthly Goals:**
  - Revenue & Profit
  - % Share
  - Volume of Clients / Contracts

- **Quarterly Goals:**
  - Revenue & Profit
  - % Share
  - Volume of Clients / Contracts

- **Annual Goals:**
  - Revenue & Profit
  - % Share
  - Volume of Clients / Contracts

Setting **Strategies**
(Achieving Objectives + Goals)

Strategies guide activities and resources across your organization to achieve the success metrics you have set and answer two questions:

1. What are your competitive advantages to achieve your goals?

2. How will you achieve our goals?

WHEN WRITING YOUR STRATEGIES THINK ABOUT

- What is needed to improve / grow core metrics?
- What is needed to give more to your end customer?
- What performance / tech gaps do you have?

EXAMPLE STRATEGIES

- Scale Direct Sales with Defined Key Accounts
- Boost Account Mngt. Team Involvement in Day to Day Sales
- Increase Use of Automation Tools for Sales & Marketing
- Launch Staff Training & Retention Programs
- Create New Products

Take First Pass At Writing Strategies

e

- Strategy 1:

- Strategy 2:

- Strategy 3:

- Strategy 4:

Setting **Measures**
(Dates & Metrics Of Success)

YOUR MEASURES ARE NUMBERS THAT DEFINE
AN ORGANIZATION'S PROGRESS TOWARD
DELIVERING A STRATEGY

Each Strategy should have two or three Measures that define whether the Strategy is effective and answer two questions:

1. What measures do you need to collect data for?
2. How are you evaluating performance of the organization, managers, employees & volunteers vs. your benchmarks?

WHEN SETTING YOUR MEASURES THINK ABOUT

- What metrics predict success?
- When should metrics be achieved?
- What items should be on a scorecard?

EXAMPLE MEASURES

- Daily: Sellers complete 5+ new biz outbounds and 5+ follow-ups
- Pipeline : Each seller to have 30 deals working each month
- Deals: Each seller to close 3 deals / Mo. at avg of $50k / 450k/ Qtr
- Weekly Booked Biz: Team to write a min. of $150,000 each week

Take First Pass At Writing Measures

- Strategy 1 MEASURES:

1-
2-
3-

- Strategy 2 MEASURES:

1-
2-
3-

- Strategy 3 MEASURES:

1-
2-
3-

- Strategy 4 MEASURES:

1-
2-
3-

Setting **Tactics**
(Actions / Projects To Do)

YOUR TACTICS ARE INDIVIDUAL PROJECTS
ASSIGNED TO SPECIFIC PEOPLE TO ACHIEVE
STRATEGIES + MEASURES

**Tactics and progress against tactics should be
updated weekly / monthly and answer two questions:**

> 1. What needs to be done to achieve your strategies?
> 2. What can you delegate to make most # of people
>   feel like owners?

WHEN SETTING YOUR TACTICS THINK ABOUT

- What needs to get done?
- What needs to be developed or built?
- Who do you need to work with?

EXAMPLE TACTICS

- Launch Monthly Customer & Prospect
  Communication
- Develop Outbound Messaging to Drive Inbound
  Interest
- Integrate CRM with email mngt. platform
- Streamline Event Registration Data Capture
- Improve Volume of Data That We Capture
- Build a Research Department

Take First Pass At Writing Tactics

• Strategy 1 TACTICS:

1-
2-
3-

• Strategy 2 TACTICS:

1-
2-
3-

• Strategy 3 TACTICS:

1-
2-
3-

• Strategy 4 TACTICS:

1-
2-
3-

Cascading Your OGSMT – For Larger Groups

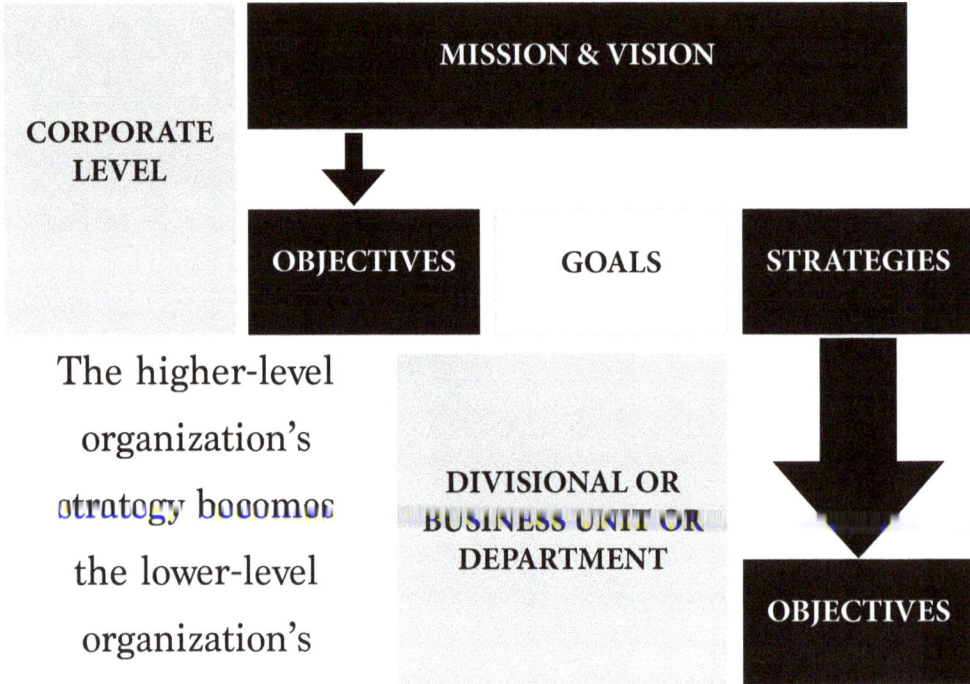

CORPORATE LEVEL

MISSION & VISION

OBJECTIVES   GOALS   **STRATEGIES**

DIVISIONAL OR BUSINESS UNIT OR DEPARTMENT

OBJECTIVES

The higher-level organization's strategy becomes the lower-level organization's objective. The higher-level organization's measures become the lower-level organization's goals and so on

A well-cascaded
OGSMT ensures
that each team's
(or an individual's)
activities are aligned
with the overall
organization's
objectives and goals

MEASURES   TACTICS

GOALS	STRATEGIES	**MEASURES**	TACTICS

**TEAM
OR
INDIVIDUAL**

	OBJECTIVES	**GOALS**	STRATEGIES, M, T..

TASK #5

USE NOTES YOU HAVE WRITTEN OUT ON THE PREVIOUS PAGES IN STEP 5 TO AUTHOR YOUR O.G.S.M.T.

• Rapid write, retreat, repeat

• Know that you might need 15-20 versions

• Then transfer your info into your OGSMT workbook!

The Five Step Process > Series of One Sheets

1. SURVEY > 2. BUSINESS CANVAS > 3.COMPETITOR GRID > 4. SWOT > 5. OGSMT

OGSMT

20XX

Mission (Purpose)

Vision (Aspiration)

	THE WHAT			THE HOW		
O - OBJECTIVES	G - GOALS	S - STRAGTEGIES	M - MEASURES	T - TACTICS	OWNER(S)	DUE DATE
What to Accomplish / Overarching, qualitative goals for the business	Quantitative Measures That Define Success	Plans to Bring Achievement of Quantitative Goals	Date or Numerical Metric of Success of Strategy	Actions / Projects Needed to Complete Strategy	Owner of Tactic	Target Date for Completion of Tactic
		S1	M1	T1	U1	D1
				T2	U2	D2
	G1		M2	T3	U3	D3
				T4	U4	D4
		S2	M3	T5	U5	D5
				T6	U6	D6
		S3	M4	T7	U7	D7
				T8	U8	D8
O2	G2		M5	T9	U9	D9
				T10	U10	D10
		S4	M6	T11	U11	D11
				T12	U12	D12
		S5	M7	T13	U13	D13
				T14	U14	D14
O3	G3		M8	T15	U15	D15
				T16	U16	D16
		S6	M9	T17	U17	D17
				T18	U18	D18

Please scan the QR code to access the Google Sheets and Excel Workbook. For Google Sheets, the file is in "View" mode so choose "File", "Copy" and then save it to your G Drive to edit

Did This Book Deliver On the Three Benefits?

01.

Access New Tools To Grow Your Revenue Mindset

02.

Learn The Five Step Process for Writing Simple but Effective Plans

03.

Integrate Relentless Preparation Into Your Routine

DGTLCORE.COM/SURVEY

AUTHOR PROFILE

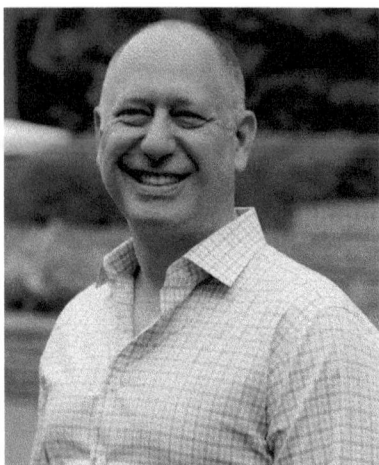

For the past 25 years Mort Greenberg has been a salesperson and sales manager for technology start-ups and larger media companies. These companies have included a variety of fund raising efforts, larger and small, to IPOs, and several mergers and acquisitions. Fighting his way up from an Account Executive to a role as a division President with 800+ employees, including 103 sellers delivering $220 million of annual revenue, you can guess there were many challenges that needed to be overcome. From the early Internet days at Excite.com he was fortunate to be part of a team that sold 5% of all ad revenue on the Internet in 1996 ($13M of $268M). He was among some of the first to create the marketplace for digital advertising. Being part of a small group tasked with rebuilding the revenue efforts for the search engine Ask Jeeves was a highlight for him and the group he worked with, right through its acquisition for $1.9 billion five years later. Learning lessons of the need for speed in decision making came from his time with Tel Aviv based Metacafe at the start of the Online video industry.

Much of his career has been about finding ways to be creative and do more with less resources. While at organizations like IAC InterActiveCorp, NBC Universal, Nokia and iHeartMedia he spent time developing systems to simplify go to market strategies. During his Nokia days he traveled the globe and learned from some of the most talented coworkers you could find in Brazil, Argentina, Mexico, England, Finland, Germany, UAE, India, Singapore and more. Along the way he launched two of his own companies, FitAd and MindFlight, and learned the hard way that start-ups are not always successful. For the past six years his time has been spent with a private equity firm to improve and grow 18 media properties in the military, defense, history and home and garden categories. The #1 lesson he has learned in the past few years is that by improving people's revenue mindset, business problems are healed and teams motivated through innovation that new revenue affords.

You can find me on most social media including LinkedIn and Twitter @MortGreenberg

REVENUE.
MINDSET.

www.ingramcontent.com/pod-product-compliance
Lightning Source LLC
Chambersburg PA
CBHW040929210326
41597CB00030B/5242